MARGARET FULTON'S
BOOK OF
VEGETARIAN COOKING

GW00598872

MARGARET FULTON'S
BOOK OF
VEGETARIAN
COOKING

octopus

CONTENTS

This edition published in 1989
by Octopus Illustrated Publishing
Michelin House
81 Fulham Road
London SW3 6RB
part of Reed International Books

Reprinted 1991,1992

ISBN 0 7064 5031 0

Produced by Mandarin Offset
Printed and bound in Hong Kong

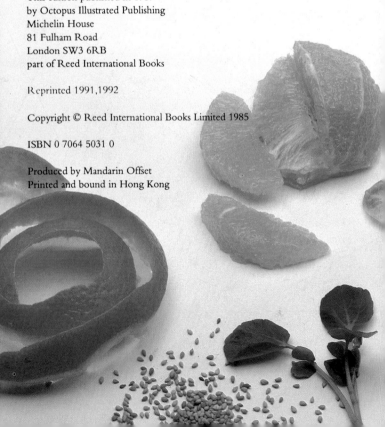

INTRODUCTION

As our knowledge of food and nutrition increases, more and more families – especially those with young adults – are turning to vegetarian meals. Fortunately, as a result of this increased interest in meatless cooking, a greater variety of unprocessed and vegetarian foods has become available at supermarkets, health food stores and shops supplying ethnic communities.

This book has been written for cooks who are reducing the amount of meat in their families' diets and want to explore the delights of vegetarian cooking. It will also appeal to ardent vegetarians, whether they are lacto-vegetarians who simply exclude meat, fish and poultry from their diet; or Vegans who also exclude dairy produce such as milk, eggs, and cheese.

I hope you find the recipes you seek and enjoy delicious and nourishing vegetarian meals.

NOTES

Standard spoon measurements are used in all recipes
1 tablespoon = one 20 ml spoon
1 teaspoon = one 5 ml spoon
All spoon measures are level.

Ovens should be preheated to the specified temperature.

Use freshly ground black pepper where pepper is specified and sea salt, if preferred, where salt is stated.

Fresh herbs are used unless otherwise stated. If unobtainable substitute a bouquet garni of the equivalent dried herbs, or use dried herbs instead but halve the quantities stated.

Metric and imperial measurements have been calculated separately. Use one set of measurements only.

Use size 55 eggs unless otherwise stated.

Ingredients marked with an asterisk are explained on pages.

WHY VEGETARIAN?

Vegetarianism is certainly a healthy way of eating. Many of our Western diseases are of recent origin and diet–related. Too great an intake of animal fats, salt and sugar leads to a dramatic increase in the incidence of heart disease, diabetes and obesity, while other diseases, such as diverticulitis and cancer of the bowel, are directly related to lack of fibre in the diet. There is also growing concern as to the effect that preservatives, flavourings and colourings have on health.

An increase in the consumption of fresh vegetables and foods rich in plant protein at the expense of animal protein helps to prevent these 'civilized diseases'.

ALTERNATIVE FOODS

Meat, poultry and fish are prime sources of the protein essential to health, so the vegetarian must seek alternative sources. These can be found in nuts, seeds, legumes (beans and pulses) and, to a lesser extent, in whole grains. These sources also contain fibre, which plays an essential part in the way the body handles the food we eat, but they do not contain the saturated animal fats which are harmful to health.

Vegetarian recipes do not necessarily require the use of whole foods, but they have been used throughout this book in preference to processed foods. Whilst individual ingredients may sometimes appear expensive, it can be cheaper to eat nuts, fruit and vegetables than meat!

When adopting this new way of eating, you must ensure that you achieve a properly balanced diet. There are four main food groups within a vegetarian diet: beans, nuts and seeds; grains; dairy produce; and fruit and vegetables. If you include something from each group in your daily diet you will be sure of getting all the nutrients you need.

PLANNING MEALS

Embarking on a new style of eating will inevitably mean more time spent in the planning and preparation of meals at first. It is in fact no more difficult to cook vegetarian food than any other, but it will take a little time to become accustomed to new methods and to know which foods are best served together.

Try to include a different grain, bean or pulse dish whenever possible so that you discover different combinations of flavours and textures. In particular, it is important to remember that you are no longer tied to the traditional 'meat and 2 veg' concept. Vegetarian cookery is a rich and varied cuisine, full of many marvellous dishes with definite characteristics. It encompasses many foreign specialities and may comprise of several equally important courses or several dishes served at once. The following guidelines are useful:

● Use wholewheat flour and pasta and brown rice – all of which have more flavour than their white equivalents.

● Breadcrumbs, preferably wholewheat, are used in many recipes and it is a good idea to keep a supply in the freezer for use at a moment's notice.

● Beans are used extensively, so cook large quantities, bag them in usable portions and freeze; they'll then be ready for use within an hour.

● Always keep the water in which you have boiled vegetables for use as a stock. For extra flavour use shoyu (see page 11), yeast extract or vegetable concentrates.

SPECIAL INGREDIENTS

Beans
Beans contain plenty of protein, iron and potassium, and they are the best source of vegetable fibre. There are more than 20 different types of peas and beans, many of which can be sprouted. The mung bean is the most common sprouted bean, producing the familiar bean sprouts.

All beans should be soaked, then drained and rapidly boiled in fresh liquid for 10 minutes at the start of cooking.

Buckwheat
Buckwheat, also known as 'saracen corn', is the seed of a herbaceous plant. It is rich in protein and iron. It is available from healthfood stores, in the form of flour, groats or roasted buckwheat called 'kasha'.

Cheese
Most hard cheeses are made with animal rennet, but a number of vegetarian cheeses are now available and many of the softer cheeses, such as cottage cheese, Ricotta and Feta, are made without rennet.

Dried Fruits
Dried fruits provide protein, iron, calcium, vitamin A, and several B vitamins. Many dried fruits, such as apricots, pears, peaches and apples, are treated with sulphur dioxide to help keep

their colour. To remove this, boil the fruit in water for 1 minute before use and discard the water. Most Australian dried fruit comes washed and tumbled dried ready to be used.

Grains

Grains or cereals are probably the most important staple food in the world. Wheat, rice, barley, oats, millet, rye, and maize are the major food grains. If eaten whole and unrefined they provide valuable fibre in the diet, as well as protein, calcium, iron, phosphorus and potassium.

Lentils

Lentils are one of the oldest crops, cultivated since prehistoric times. They are grown all over the Middle East and India. Of the many varieties, the most common are the green or continental lentils, and brown or split red lentils. They do not need to be soaked before use, though it will shorten the cooking time if they are. Split red lentils are shelled and have therefore lost some of their fibre.

ABOVE: *Red kidney beans, black eye beans, mung beans, chick peas, black beans, butter beans, buckwheat, buckwheat flour, Ricotta cheese, chèvre.*
BELOW: *Prunes, dried apples, dried apricots, figs, pot barley, rolled oats, bulgur wheat, wholewheat, red lentils, green lentils.*

Nuts and Seeds
Nuts and seeds are a high protein food, rich in B vitamins and minerals. Their high fat content is rich in linoleic acid.

Oils and Fats
Oils are one of the essentials of our diet, containing lecithin, vitamins A, E and K, and minerals. Fats and oils can be divided into three kinds: saturated, mono-unsaturated and polyunsaturated. Animal fats, which are solid at room temperature, are high in saturated fats. Excessive consumption of these fats is associated with heart disease. Most vegetable oils are high in polyunsaturated oils. These are preferable because they tend to lower the level of cholesterol in the blood. Polyunsaturated oils include safflower, sunflower, sesame and maize oil. Olive oil is mono-unsaturated and can be regarded as neutral. Margarine, despite its labelling 'high in polyunsaturates', may contain 50 per cent saturated fat.

Sesame Salt
Sesame salt or 'Gomasio' is a good alternative to salt. It is available in healthfood shops but can be made by grinding 5 parts roasted sesame seeds with 1 part salt.

Sea Vegetables
Seaweed is one of the oldest crops. There are many varieties, the most common being Arame, Kombu, Wakame, Dulse and Nori. They are very high in vitamins, essential amino acids and trace elements, especially iodine.

Agar Agar is obtained from several different seaweeds and is used as a substitute for animal gelatine.

Soy Sauce/Shoyu
Naturally fermented soy sauce made from soya beans with wheat or barley is known as 'shoyu'. The manufactured soy sauce usually contains sugar and other additives. Shoyu makes an excellent flavouring for soups, stews, sauces and dressings and as it is quite salty allows you to cut down on added salt. Soy sauce can be used but the flavour will not be as strong.

Tahini
Tahini is a sesame seed paste widely used in the Middle East. It is useful as a flavouring in dips and sauces and can be used as a binding agent in rissoles and nut roasts.

Tofu
Tofu is soya bean curd. Its high protein content makes it a nutritional substitute for meat, fish and dairy products. It is also rich in iron, calcium and B vitamins. Tofu is a versatile ingredient: it can be stir-fried, deep-fried, marinated and added to dressings and sauces. It is available from healthfood and Asian stores as lightly pressed 'silken tofu', and 'firm tofu' which is more heavily pressed. Regular tofu has a texture in between the two.

Yogurt
Yogurt is a popular fermented milk product. It is very easily digested, especially goats' milk yogurt, and people who are allergic or sensitive to milk are often able to tolerate yogurt.

ABOVE: *Brazil nuts, hazelnuts, cashews, pumpkin seeds, roasted sesame seeds, whole mixed nuts, safflower oil, maize oil, olive oil, sesame salt, sesame seeds.*
BELOW: *Wakame, Nori, Arame, soy sauce, tahini, tofu, yogurt.*

SOUPS AND STARTERS

CHILLED YOGURT AND MINT SOUP

300 g natural yogurt
2/3 cup tomato juice
1¼ cups milk
1 clove garlic, crushed
1 small cucumber, peeled
    and finely diced
2 tablespoons chopped
    mint
salt and pepper
mint sprigs to garnish

Place the yogurt and tomato juice in a bowl and mix together thoroughly. Stir in the milk, garlic, cucumber, most of the chopped mint, and salt and pepper to taste. Chill for 2 hours.

Pour the soup into a tureen, and sprinkle with the remaining mint. Garnish with mint sprigs to serve.
Serves 4

CHESTNUT SOUP

1 tablespoon oil
1 onion, chopped
2 celery sticks, chopped
2½ cups water
bouquet garni
salt and pepper
1 × 439 g can
    unsweetened chestnut
    purée
1¼ cups milk
1 teaspoon lemon juice
TO SERVE:
4 tablespoons sour cream
1 tablespoon chopped
    parsley

Heat the oil in a pan, add the onion and fry until softened. Add the celery, water, bouquet garni, and salt and pepper to taste, cover and simmer gently for 20 minutes. Add the chestnut purée and milk and simmer for 10 minutes. Remove the bouquet garni.

Cool slightly, then place in an electric blender or food processor. Add the lemon juice and blend until smooth. Return to the pan to heat through. Pour into a warmed soup tureen and swirl the sour cream on top. Sprinkle with the parsley to serve.
Serves 6

LENTIL AND CELERY SOUP

2 tablespoons oil
1 onion, chopped
3 celery sticks, chopped
1 clove garlic, crushed
1 cup red lentils
4 cups water
bouquet garni
salt and pepper

Heat the oil in a large pan, add the onion and fry until softened. Add the remaining ingredients, with salt and pepper to taste. Bring to the boil, cover and simmer for 30 to 35 minutes, stirring occasionally.

Check the seasoning and remove the bouquet garni. Pour into a warmed soup tureen to serve.
Serves 6

MINESTRONE

2 tablespoons oil
2 onions, chopped
2 carrots, chopped
3 celery sticks, chopped
1 leek, sliced
2 cloves garlic, crushed
125 g (4 oz) green
    cabbage, shredded
bouquet garni
10 cups water
4 tablespoons tomato paste
4 tomatoes, skinned and
    chopped
2 tablespoons chopped
    parsley
¼ cup wholemeal pasta
salt and pepper
TO SERVE:
grated Parmesan cheese

Heat the oil in a large pan, add the onions and fry until softened. Add the carrots, celery, leek and garlic, cover and cook gently for 10 minutes. Add the remaining ingredients, with salt and pepper to taste, and bring to the boil. Cover and simmer gently for 30 to 40 minutes, until all the vegetables are tender. Remove the bouquet garni.

Pour into a warmed soup tureen and serve with grated Parmesan cheese.

Serves 8

BARLEY AND VEGETABLE BROTH

¼ cup pot barley
2 tablespoons oil
1 large onion, chopped
2 celery sticks, thinly
    sliced
3 carrots, thinly sliced
2 cloves garlic, crushed
1 turnip, chopped
1 cup green beans, cut into
    2.5 cm (1 inch) lengths
bouquet garni
6 cups water or vegetable
    stock
1 tablespoon shoyu*
salt and pepper
4 tomatoes, skinned and
    chopped
2 tablespoons chopped
    parsley

Soak the barley in cold water to cover for 1 hour. Drain well and set aside.

Heat the oil in a pan, add the onion and fry until softened. Add the celery, carrots, garlic and turnip. Cover and cook gently for 10 minutes, shaking the pan occasionally.

Add the soaked barley, green beans, bouquet garni, water or stock, shoyu, and salt and pepper to taste. Cover and simmer for 45 minutes, until tender.

Add the tomatoes and parsley and cook for a further 10 minutes. Check the seasoning and remove the bouquet garni. Pour into a warmed soup tureen to serve.

Serves 6 to 8

NOTE: Pot barley is the wholefood equivalent to pearl barley because it doesn't have the husk removed.

PEA SOUP

1 tablespoon oil
1 onion, chopped
1 clove garlic, crushed
2 celery sticks, chopped
1½ cups dried blue boiling
    peas, soaked overnight
6 cups water
bouquet garni
salt and pepper
mint sprig to garnish

Heat the oil in a large pan, add the onion and cook until softened. Add the garlic and celery and cook for 5 minutes, stirring occasionally.

Drain the peas and add to the pan with the water, bouquet garni, and salt and pepper to taste. Cover and boil rapidly for 10 minutes, then simmer gently for 2 to 3 hours, until the peas are soft. Remove the bouquet garni.

Cool slightly, then place half the soup in an electric blender or food processor and work to a smooth purée. Return to the pan. Repeat with the remaining soup. Reheat the soup gently, adding a little more water if it is too thick. Pour into a warmed soup tureen and garnish with mint to serve.
Serves 4 to 6

BEAN SOUP

1¼ cups haricot beans,
    soaked overnight
5 cups water
salt and pepper
2 tablespoons olive oil
1 large onion, chopped
2 celery sticks, sliced
2 cloves garlic, crushed
2 tablespoons chopped
    parsley

Drain the beans thoroughly, then place in a pan with the water. Cover, bring to the boil and boil rapidly for 10 minutes, then simmer for 1 to 1½ hours until soft, adding a little salt towards the end of cooking. Drain, reserving the cooking liquid.

Heat the oil in a large pan, add the onion, celery and garlic and fry for 5 minutes.

Place half the beans and 2½ cups of the reserved liquid in an electric blender or food processor and work to a purée. Add to the onion and celery with remaining beans and bring to the boil. Add salt and pepper to taste and cook for 30 minutes.

Pour into a warmed soup tureen and sprinkle with the parsley to serve.
Serves 4 to 6

AVOCADO WITH RASPBERRY VINAIGRETTE

2 avocados, halved and
    stoned
1 tablespoon lemon juice
125 g (4 oz) raspberries
2 tablespoons olive oil
1 tablespoon wine vinegar
½ teaspoon clear honey
salt and pepper
fennel leaves to garnish
    (optional)

Peel each avocado half and place cut side down on a serving plate. Slice through the avocados lengthwise, then separate the slices slightly. Brush lightly with the lemon juice.

Press the raspberries through a nylon sieve to remove the seeds, then mix with the oil, vinegar, honey and salt and pepper to taste. Spoon a little around each avocado and serve immediately, garnished with fennel.
Serves 4

STUFFED MUSHROOMS

500 g (1 lb) mushrooms
2 tablespoons oil
2 cloves garlic, crushed
1 tablespoon each chopped
    chives and parsley
1 egg yolk
2 tablespoons cream
1 cup wholewheat
    breadcrumbs
½ teaspoon chopped
    thyme
salt and pepper
SAUCE:
30 g (1 oz) margarine
¼ cup wholemeal flour
1¼ cups milk
½ cup grated Cheddar
    cheese
TO FINISH:
1 tablespoon grated
    Parmesan cheese
1 tablespoon wholewheat
    breadcrumbs, toasted
thyme sprigs to garnish

Remove the stalks from 16 of the mushrooms. Heat the oil in a frying pan, add the mushroom caps, rounded side down, and fry for 1 to 2 minutes to soften. Place rounded side down on 4 individual ovenproof dishes.

Chop the stalks and remaining mushrooms and mix with the remaining ingredients, seasoning with salt and pepper to taste. Place a spoonful in each mushroom cap.

To make the sauce, melt the margarine in a small pan and stir in the flour. Remove from the heat and stir in the milk until blended. Cook gently, stirring constantly, until thickened. Add salt and pepper to taste, then stir in the Cheddar cheese. Spoon over the mushrooms.

Mix the Parmesan cheese and breadcrumbs together, then sprinkle over the mushrooms. Cook in a preheated moderate oven, 180°C (350°F), for 20 minutes, until golden. Serve immediately, garnished with thyme.
Serves 4

FALAFEL

1¼ cups chick peas,
    soaked overnight
4 spring onions, chopped
2 cloves garlic, chopped
3 tablespoons water
4 large parsley sprigs
½ teaspoon ground cumin
1 teaspoon ground
    coriander
salt and pepper
oil for deep-frying

Drain the peas and place in an electric blender or food processor with the spring onions, garlic, water and parsley. Work to a purée, scraping down the sides when necessary. Stir in the remaining ingredients, with salt and pepper to taste, then turn into a bowl and leave for 1 to 2 hours and dry out slightly.

Form the mixture into walnut-sized balls and flatten slightly. Heat the oil in a deep-fryer, add the falafel and fry for about 4 minutes, until golden. Drain on kitchen paper.

Serve hot with Piquante Sauce (see page 93).

Serves 6

BABA GHANOUSH

This is a popular dish in the Middle East where it is served quite often. If possible, grill the eggplant over charcoal as this gives them a delicious smoky flavour that blends well with tahini.

2 large eggplant
2 cloves garlic, crushed
4 tablespoons tahini* (see
    below)
juice of 1 lemon
½ teaspoon ground cumin
2 tablespoons chopped
    parsley
salt and pepper
TO GARNISH:
2 black olives, halved and
    stoned

Prick the eggplant all over with a fork, cut in half and place, cut side down, on a grill pan rack. Place under a preheated low grill until the skins are black and start to blister and the flesh feels soft. Peel and wash the eggplant and squeeze out as much of the juice as possible, as this is rather bitter.

Chop the eggplant flesh, place in an electric blender or food processor with the garlic and blend to a purée. Add the tahini and lemon juice alternately, blending between each addition. Turn into a bowl and stir in the cumin, parsley, and salt and pepper to taste.

Turn into a shallow serving dish and garnish with the olives. Serve with wholewheat pitta bread.

Serves 6

NOTE: Tahini is a sesame seed paste. It is available from healthfood stores and delicatessens.

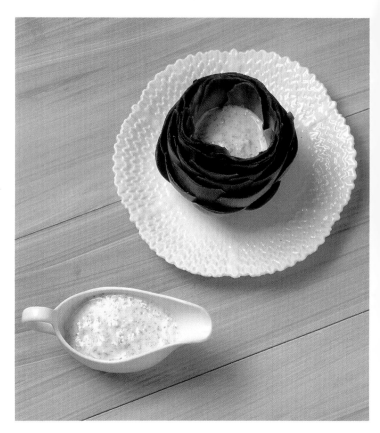

ARTICHOKE WITH HERB MAYONNAISE

4 globe artichokes
salt
4 tablespoons Green Herb
   Dressing (see page 92)
4 tablespoons fromage
   frais or Ricotta cheese

Trim the points of the artichoke leaves square with scissors and cut off the stalk to level the base.

Place in a large pan of boiling salted water and cook for 35 to 45 minutes, until one of the leaves can be pulled out easily. Place upside down in a collander to drain and cool.

Gently ease the outer leaves so that you can remove the centre purple-tinged leaves and the 'choke', which is inedible; take care not to remove any of the 'fond' underneath.

Fold the dressing into the Ricotta and spoon a tablespoon into the bottom of each artichoke. Place on individual dishes and serve the remaining herb sauce separately.
Serves 4

PEANUT DIP WITH CRUDITÉS

2 tablespoons sunflower
    oil
1 onion, finely chopped
2 cloves garlic, crushed
1/2 teaspoon chilli powder
1 teaspoon ground cumin
1 teaspoon ground
    coriander
4 tablespoons crunchy
    peanut butter
1/2 cup water
1 teaspoon shoyu*
1 teaspoon lemon juice
CRUDITÉS:
1 small cauliflower
1 bunch of radishes
1 red pepper, cored and
    seeded
6 celery sticks
6 carrots

Heat the oil in a pan, add the onion
and fry until softened. Add the garlic
and spices, stir and cook for 1 minute.
Mix in the peanut butter, then
gradually blend in the water, stirring
until thickened. Add the shoyu and
lemon juice and leave to cool.

Break the cauliflower into florets
and halve the radishes if large. Cut
the remaining vegetables into long
thin pieces.

Turn the dip into a dish, place on a
large plate and surround with the
vegetables.
Serves 6

HUMMOUS

1½ cups chick peas,
    soaked overnight
⅔ cup tahini*
3 cloves garlic
juice of 1-2 lemons
salt and pepper
TO FINISH:
1 tablespoon olive oil
    blended with 1 teaspoon
    paprika
1 teaspoon chopped
    parsley

Drain the chick peas, place in a pan and cover with cold water. Bring to the boil, cover and boil rapidly for 10 minutes, then simmer gently for 1½ to 2 hours, until soft; the time will vary depending on the age and quality of the peas. Drain, reserving 1½ cups of the liquid.

Place the chick peas in an electric blender or food processor and add the remaining ingredients, seasoning with salt and pepper to taste, and enough of the reserved liquid to blend to a soft creamy paste.

Turn into a shallow serving dish, dribble over the blended oil and sprinkle with the parsley. Serve with pitta bread.

Serves 8 to 10

NOTE: This will keep for up to 1 week, covered in the refrigerator.

FLAGEOLET VINAIGRETTE

1¼ cups flageolet beans,
    soaked overnight
salt
4 tablespoons French
    Dressing (see page 92)
1 red pepper, cored, seeded
    and chopped
4 spring onions, chopped
1 tablespoon chopped
    mixed herbs: parsley,
    thyme and mint
2 celery sticks, thinly
    sliced

Drain the beans, place in a pan and cover with cold water. Bring to the boil and boil rapidly for 10 minutes. Cover and simmer for about 1 hour, until tender, adding a little salt towards the end of cooking. Drain thoroughly and place in a bowl.

Pour over the dressing while still warm and mix well. Leave to cool, then add the remaining ingredients. Toss thoroughly and transfer to a shallow dish to serve.

Serves 4

TZATSIKI

500 g natural yogurt
    (preferably Greek)
1 cucumber, peeled and
    grated
3 cloves garlic, crushed
salt and pepper
1 tablespoon chopped mint

Mix the yogurt with a fork until smooth. Drain the cucumber, then add to the yogurt with the garlic, and salt and pepper to taste. Chill for 2 hours, then turn into a serving bowl and sprinkle with the mint. Serve with wholewheat pitta bread.

Serves 6

SALADS

CASHEW COLESLAW

250 g (8 oz) firm white
   cabbage, shredded
3 celery sticks, sliced
3 red-skinned eating
   apples, cored and thinly
   sliced
4 spring onions, sliced
½ cup cashew nuts,
   toasted and split
2 tablespoons chopped
   parsley
⅔ cup mayonnaise
2 tablespoons natural
   yogurt

Place the cabbage, celery, apples,
spring onions, cashews and parsley in
a mixing bowl.

Mix the mayonnaise and yogurt
together, then pour over the salad and
toss thoroughly. Transfer to a salad
bowl to serve.

Serves 6 to 8

RED BEAN AND BEANSHOOT SALAD

1 cup red kidney beans,
   soaked overnight
salt
125 g (4 oz) mushrooms,
   sliced
5 tablespoons Vinaigrette
   Dressing (see page 92)
250 g (8 oz) beanshoots
1 red pepper, cored, seeded
   and thinly sliced
2 tablespoons toasted
   sunflower seeds
2 tablespoons chopped
   parsley

Drain the beans, place in a pan and
cover with cold water. Bring to the
boil, cover and boil rapidly for
10 minutes, then simmer for
45 minutes to 1 hour, until tender;
add a little salt towards the end of
cooking.

Drain the beans and place in a bowl
with the mushrooms. Pour over the
dressing and mix thoroughly. Leave
to cool.

Add the remaining ingredients and
toss well. Transfer to a shallow dish
to serve.

Serves 6

CELERIAC AND EGG SALAD

500 g (1 lb) celeriac
4 tablespoons Vinaigrette
 Dressing (see page 92)
2 hard-boiled eggs
1 tablespoon chopped
 parsley

Grate the celeriac finely and place in a mixing bowl. Pour over the dressing, toss thoroughly and leave for 1 hour.

Shred the egg whites finely and mix with the celeriac. Place in a shallow serving dish and sieve the egg yolks over the top. Sprinkle with the parsley to serve.
Serves 4

CHICORY AND SESAME SALAD

3 heads of chicory
2 oranges
1 bunch of watercress
1/4 cup sesame seeds,
 toasted
3 tablespoons olive oil
1 tablespoon lemon juice
salt and pepper

Cut the chicory diagonally into 1 cm (1/2 inch) slices and place in a bowl. Remove the peel and pith from the oranges and cut the flesh into segments, holding the fruit over the bowl so that any juice is included.

Divide the watercress into sprigs and add to the bowl with the sesame seeds.

Whisk together the oil, lemon juice, and salt and pepper to taste, then pour over the salad and toss thoroughly. Transfer to a salad bowl to serve.
Serves 4 to 6

CAULIFLOWER AND CRESS SALAD

500 g (1 lb) cauliflower,
 broken into florets
salt
1 carton mustard and
 cress, trimmed or 1 cup
 alfalfa shoots
25 g (1 oz) pumpkin
 seeds
3 tablespoons French
 Dressing (see page 92)

Cook the cauliflower in boiling salted water for 1 minute; drain and leave to cool completely. Place in a bowl with the remaining ingredients and toss thoroughly. Transfer to a shallow dish to serve.
Serves 4
NOTE: Pumpkin seeds and alfalfa shoots are available from healthfood stores.

SPRING CABBAGE AND PEPPER SALAD

250 g (8 oz) spring
   cabbage, very finely
   shredded
4 tablespoons Shoyu
   Dressing (see page 92)
3 celery sticks, sliced
4 spring onions, chopped
1 red pepper, cored, seeded
   and diced

Place the spring cabbage in a bowl
with the dressing, toss thoroughly
and leave to marinate for 1 hour. Add
the remaining ingredients and toss
thoroughly. Transfer to a salad bowl
to serve.
Serves 4 to 6

ARTICHOKE VINAIGRETTE

500 g (1 lb) Jerusalem
   artichokes, scrubbed
3 tablespoons French
   Dressing (see page 92)
1 tablespoon chopped
   parsley
1 tablespoon pumpkin
   seeds
1 teaspoon lemon juice

Grate the artichokes coarsely and
place in a mixing bowl with the
remaining ingredients. Toss
thoroughly and leave for 1 hour.
Transfer to a shallow serving dish to
serve.
Serves 4 to 6
NOTE: Pumpkin seeds are available
from healthfood stores.

TOMATO AND YOGURT SALAD

A delicious refreshing salad accompaniment to serve in the summer – perfect for 'al fresco' meals.

300 g natural yogurt
2 tablespoons chopped basil
salt and pepper
500 g (1 lb) tomatoes, skinned and cut into wedges

Place the yogurt in a bowl, add the chopped basil, and salt and pepper to taste and mix well. Stir in the tomatoes, then transfer to a shallow serving dish.

Chill in the refrigerator for about 30 minutes before serving.
Serves 4 to 6

Variation: If basil is unobtainable, replace it with 1 tablespoon chopped fresh coriander leaves. This salad makes an excellent accompaniment to serve with curries and other hot spicy dishes.

TABBOULEH

¼ cup bulgur wheat
1 cup chopped parsley
3 tablespoons chopped
    mint
4 spring onions, chopped
½ cucumber, finely diced
2 tablespoons olive oil
juice of 1 lemon
salt and pepper

Soak the Bulgur wheat in cold water for 1 hour. Line a sieve with muslin and tip the wheat into it. Lift out the muslin and squeeze out as much moisture as possible.

Place the wheat in a bowl and add the remaining ingredients, seasoning with salt and pepper to taste. Toss thoroughly, then transfer to a shallow dish to serve.

Serves 4

NOTE: Bulgur wheat is available from healthfood stores.

ADUKI BEAN SALAD

250 g (8 oz) aduki beans,
    soaked overnight
salt and pepper
4 tablespoons Ginger
    Dressing (see page 92)
6 spring onions, chopped
4 tomatoes, skinned and
    chopped
3 celery sticks, sliced
2 tablespoons chopped
    parsley

Drain the beans, place in a pan of boiling salted water and boil rapidly for 10 minutes. Cover and cook for 30 to 35 minutes or until tender. Drain well and mix with the dressing while still warm. Leave to cool.

Add the remaining ingredients, seasoning with salt and pepper to taste. Mix thoroughly and transfer to a shallow dish to serve.

Serves 6

NOTE: Aduki beans are a small type of red kidney bean. If unobtainable, use kidney beans instead.

BUCKWHEAT AND CORN SALAD

¾ cup toasted buckwheat*
salt
4 tablespoons Ginger
    Dressing (see page 92)
1 × 300 g can sweetcorn,
    drained
1 green pepper, cored,
    seeded and chopped
3 tomatoes, skinned and
    chopped
2 tablespoons chopped
    parsley
¼ cup toasted sunflower
    seeds

Place the buckwheat in a pan of boiling salted water, cover and simmer gently for 15 minutes. Drain thoroughly and place in a bowl with the dressing.

Add the remaining ingredients and toss thoroughly. Transfer to a shallow dish to serve.

Serves 4-6

NOTE: Buckwheat is available from healthfood stores.

POTATO AND EGG MAYONNAISE

500 g (1 lb) waxy (salad)
    potatoes
salt
2 tablespoons French
    Dressing (see page 92)
4 spring onions, sliced
4 hard-boiled eggs,
    chopped
2 dill pickles, chopped
3 tablespoons mayonnaise
3 tablespoons natural
    yogurt
1 tablespoon chopped
    fennel to garnish

Cook the potatoes in their skins in
boiling salted water until tender.
Drain well, chop roughly and place in
a bowl. Pour over the dressing while
still warm, toss thoroughly and leave
to cool. Add the spring onions, eggs
and dill pickles.

Mix together the mayonnaise,
yogurt and 2 tablespoons juice from
the dill pickles until smooth. Pour
over the salad and mix thoroughly.
Transfer to a shallow dish and
sprinkle with the fennel to serve.
Serves 4

Swedish Potato Salad: Omit the
hard-boiled eggs. Substitute with
1 cup chopped cooked beetroot.

POTATO AND MINT VINAIGRETTE

500 g (1 lb) new potatoes
salt
3 tablespoons French
   Dressing (see page 92)
3 tablespoons chopped
   mint
1 bunch radishes, thinly
   sliced

Cook the potatoes in their skins in boiling salted water until tender. Drain well and mix with the dressing while still warm, then leave to cool.

Add the chopped mint and radishes and mix well. Transfer to a salad bowl to serve.

Serves 4

Potato and Onion Vinaigrette:
Omit the mint and radishes from the above recipe. Substitute with 6 chopped spring onions.

BROWN RICE AND HAZELNUT SALAD

1 cup brown rice
salt
2/3 cup hazelnuts, chopped
 and toasted
1 red pepper, cored, seeded
 and diced
6 spring onions, finely
 sliced
3 celery sticks, chopped
60 g (2 oz) button
 mushrooms, sliced
4 tablespoons French
 Dressing (see page 92)
3 tablespoons chopped
 parsley

Cook the rice in boiling salted water for 30 to 40 minutes, until tender. Rinse and drain well.

Place in a bowl with the remaining ingredients and toss thoroughly. Transfer to a shallow dish to serve.
Serves 6 to 8

BULGUR WHEAT VINAIGRETTE

1/2 cup bulgur wheat
4 tomatoes, skinned and
 chopped
1/3 cup black olives,
 halved and stoned
1 celery stick, thinly sliced
4 spring onions, chopped
2 tablespoons chopped
 parsley
2 tablespoons toasted
 sunflower seeds
3 tablespoons French
 Dressing (see page 92)

Soak the Bulgur wheat in cold water for 1 hour. Line a sieve with muslin and tip the wheat into it. Lift out the muslin and squeeze out as much moisture as possible.

Place the wheat in a bowl, add the remaining ingredients and mix well. Transfer to a shallow dish to serve.
Serves 4
NOTE: Bulgur wheat is available from healthfood stores and Greek delicatessens.

WHOLEWHEAT SALAD

1 cup wheat, soaked
 overnight
salt
6 tablespoons Shoyu
 Dressing (see page 92)
1 red pepper, cored, seeded
 and chopped
1/4 cup raisins
2 celery sticks, diced
2 tablespoons chopped
 parsley

Drain the wheat thoroughly. Place in a pan, cover with lightly salted water, bring to the boil and simmer for 1 to 1½ hours; drain well. Mix with the dressing while still warm, then leave to cool.

Add the remaining ingredients, toss well, then transfer to a shallow dish to serve.
Serves 4 to 6

VEGETABLE DISHES

VEGETABLE RISOTTO

4 tablespoons oil
1 onion, chopped
1 cup brown rice
3 cloves garlic, crushed
2½ cups water
1 teaspoon salt
2 celery sticks, thinly
  sliced
1 red pepper, cored, seeded
  and diced
250 g (8 oz) button
  mushrooms, sliced
1 × 440 g can red kidney
  beans, drained
3 tablespoons chopped
  parsley
1 tablespoon shoyu*
60 g (2 oz) roasted
  cashew nuts
chopped parsley to garnish

Heat 2 tablespoons of the oil in a pan, add the onion and fry until softened. Add the rice and 2 cloves garlic and cook, stirring, for 2 minutes. Add the water and salt and bring to the boil, stirring. Cover and simmer gently for 35 to 40 minutes, until all the water has been absorbed.

Heat the remaining oil in a frying pan, add the celery and red pepper and fry for 5 minutes, until softened. Add the mushrooms and remaining garlic and fry for 3 minutes.

Add the cooked rice, kidney beans, parsley, shoyu and nuts. Cook, stirring to mix, until the beans are heated through. Serve garnished with parsley, and accompanied by a green salad.

Serves 4

This is a Provençale family dish which takes its name from the heavy earthenware dish in which it is cooked.

3 tablespoons olive oil
1 onion, chopped
2 cloves garlic, crushed
500 g (1 lb) zucchini,
    chopped
250 g (8 oz) spinach,
    cooked, drained and
    chopped
3 tablespoons brown rice,
    cooked
3 eggs, beaten
1/2 cup grated Gruyère
    cheese
salt and pepper
1 tablespoon fresh
    wholewheat
    breadcrumbs
1 tablespoon grated
    Parmesan cheese

Heat the oil in a frying pan, add the onion and cook until softened. Add the garlic and zucchini and cook for 5 minutes, stirring occasionally. Stir in the spinach, rice, eggs, Gruyère cheese, and salt and pepper to taste and mix well.

Turn into a greased 5 cup earthenware gratin dish and sprinkle with the breadcrumbs and Parmesan cheese.

Bake in a preheated moderate oven, 180°C (350°F), for 35 minutes, until golden.

Serve with salad and wholewheat bread.

Serves 4

STIR-FRIED VEGETABLES WITH TOFU

3 tablespoons shoyu*
3 tablespoons dry sherry
1 cm (½ inch) piece root
    ginger, peeled and
    finely chopped
2 cloves garlic, crushed
250 g (8 oz) firm tofu*
about 2 tablespoons
    sesame oil
1 large onion, sliced
185 g (6 oz) snow peas,
    topped, tailed and
    halved
1 red pepper, cored, seeded
    and sliced
185 g (6 oz) button
    mushrooms, sliced
500 g (1 lb) beanshoots
2 tablespoons sesame
    seeds, toasted

Mix the shoyu, sherry, chopped
ginger and garlic together in a bowl.
Cut the tofu into cubes and add to the
bowl, stirring to coat completely.
Leave to marinate for 1 hour, then
drain, reserving the marinade.

Heat the oil in a large wok, add the
tofu cubes and stir-fry for about
2 minutes, until beginning to brown
on all sides. Remove with a slotted
spoon and keep warm.

Reheat the oil, adding a little
more if necessary. Add the onion and
stir-fry for 2 minutes. Add the
snow peas and red pepper and stir-fry
for 2 minutes. Add the mushrooms,
beanshoots and reserved marinade
and stir-fry for 2 minutes, until
heated through.

Lightly stir in the tofu, then turn
onto a warmed serving dish. Sprinkle
with the sesame seeds to serve.
Serves 4

VEGETABLE CRUMBLE

1 cauliflower, broken into
  florets
salt
2 tablespoons oil
3 tablespoons wholewheat
  flour
1½ cups milk
1 × 300 g can sweetcorn,
  drained
2 tablespoons chopped
  parsley
1 cup grated matured
  Cheddar cheese

TOPPING:
½ cup wholemeal flour
30 g (1 oz) margarine
½ cup rolled oats
¼ cup chopped almonds

Cook the cauliflower in boiling salted water for 5 minutes. Drain, reserving the water.

Heat the oil in the same pan and stir in the flour. Remove from the heat, add the milk, stirring until blended. Add ⅔ cup of the reserved cooking liquid, bring to the boil and cook for 3 minutes, until thickened. Stir in the sweetcorn, parsley and half the cheese. Gently fold in the cauliflower and turn into a 7 cup ovenproof dish.

For the topping, place the flour in a bowl and rub in the margarine until the mixture resembles fine bread-crumbs. Add the oats, almonds and remaining cheese. Sprinkle over the vegetable mixture and bake in a pre-heated moderately hot oven, 190°C (375°F), for 30 minutes, until golden brown and crisp.

Serves 4-6

SPINACH LATTICE FLAN

2 tablespoons oil
1 large onion, chopped
2 cloves garlic, crushed
500 g (1 lb) frozen
  chopped spinach,
  thawed and drained
2 eggs
½ teaspoon ground
  nutmeg
250 g (8 oz) Ricotta or
  cottage cheese
½ cup grated Parmesan
  cheese
salt and pepper
WHOLEMEAL
  SHORTCRUST PASTRY:
2 cups wholemeal flour
1 cup plain flour
185 g (6 oz) margarine
3-4 tablespoons iced water
beaten egg to glaze

Heat the oil in a pan and fry the onion
until softened. Add the garlic and
spinach and cook gently for
10 minutes, stirring occasionally.
Cool slightly then beat in the eggs,
nutmeg, cheeses, and salt and pepper
to taste.

To make the pastry, place the
flours in a mixing bowl and rub in the
margarine until the mixture
resembles breadcrumbs. Add enough
water to mix to a firm dough, then
turn onto a floured surface and knead
lightly until smooth. Cut off two
thirds of the pastry, roll out thinly
and use to line a 23 cm (9 inch) flan
dish, leaving it overlapping the side.

Spread the filling evenly in the
pastry case. Moisten pastry edge.
Roll out remaining pastry and cut
into 5 mm (¼ inch) strips. Arrange in
a lattice design over the filling and
press the edges to secure. Brush with
egg and bake in a preheated
moderately hot oven, 200°C (400°F),
for 45 to 50 minutes, until golden.
Serve warm or cold with a crisp
mixed salad.
Serves 6

PROVENÇALE PANCAKES

PANCAKE BATTER:
½ cup buckwheat flour*
½ cup plain flour
pinch of salt
1 egg, beaten
1¼ cups milk
1 tablespoon oil

FILLING:
2 tablespoons olive oil
1 onion, chopped
2 cloves garlic, crushed
1 green or red pepper,
    cored, seeded and
    chopped
1 small eggplant, chopped
4 large tomatoes, skinned
    and chopped
1 tablespoon tomato paste
salt and pepper to taste

TO FINISH:
30 g (1 oz) margarine,
    melted
2 tablespoons grated
    Parmesan cheese

Place the flours and salt in a bowl and make a well in the centre. Add the egg, then gradually stir in half the milk and the oil. Beat thoroughly until smooth. Add the remaining milk.

Heat a 15 cm (6 inch) omelet pan and add a few drops of oil. Pour in 1 to 2 tablespoons of the batter, lifting the pan to coat the bottom evenly. Cook until the underside is brown, then turn over and cook for 10 seconds. Turn onto a warmed plate. Repeat with the remaining batter, making 12 pancakes. Stack interleaved with greaseproof paper.

For the filling, heat the oil in a pan and cook onion until softened. Add the garlic, pepper and eggplant and fry for 10 minutes, stirring occasionally. Add remaining ingredients, cover and cook for 15 minutes.

Divide filling between pancakes, roll up and place in an oiled shallow ovenproof dish. Top with the margarine and cheese. Bake in a preheated moderately hot oven, 190°C (375°F), for 15 minutes. Serve immediately.
Serves 4

43

SPINACH AND POTATO PATTIES

1 tablespoon oil
1 onion, chopped
1 clove garlic, crushed
250 g (8 oz) frozen
    chopped spinach,
    thawed and drained
500 g (1 lb) potatoes,
    boiled and mashed
1/4 teaspoon ground
    nutmeg
1 cup grated Cheddar
    cheese
salt and pepper
wholewheat flour for
    coating
oil for shallow-frying

Heat the oil in a pan, add the onion and garlic and fry until softened. Squeeze the spinach dry and add to the pan with the potato, nutmeg, cheese, and salt and pepper to taste; mix thoroughly. Shape the mixture into 8 balls, using dampened hands, and flatten slightly.

Place some flour in a polythene bag, add the patties one at a time and shake to coat completely.

Fry in hot shallow oil for 2 minutes on each side, until golden brown.

Serve with salad and crusty bread.
Serves 3 to 4

STUFFED SPINACH LEAVES

12 large spinach leaves,
    stalks removed
salt and pepper
1 tablespoon oil
1 onion, chopped
2 cloves garlic, crushed
250 g (8 oz) mushrooms,
    chopped
3/4 cup wholewheat
    breadcrumbs
1 tablespoon chopped
    mixed herbs, e.g.
    parsley, thyme and
    marjoram
1 egg, beaten
SAUCE:
2 egg yolks
1 tablespoon lemon juice

Put the spinach in a large pan with 1 1/4 cups salted water and boil for 2 minutes. Drain, reserving the liquid. Rinse under cold water, then place on kitchen paper and pat dry.

Heat the oil in a pan, add the onion and fry until softened. Add garlic and mushrooms and cook for 5 minutes. Stir in the breadcrumbs, herbs, egg, and salt and pepper to taste.

Place 1 tablespoon of the mixture in the centre of each spinach leaf, fold in both sides and roll up carefully.

Lay the spinach rolls in a shallow ovenproof dish and pour over 2/3 cup of the reserved liquid. Cover with foil and bake in a preheated moderately hot oven, 190°C (375°F), for 45 minutes. Strain and reserve juices; keep rolls warm.

For the sauce, whisk the egg yolks with the lemon juice in a heatproof bowl over a pan of simmering water. Add reserved cooking juices and stir for about 5 minutes, until thickened. Season with salt and pepper and pour over the spinach rolls. Serve as an accompaniment or starter.
Serves 4

MUSHROOM GOUGÈRE

CHOUX PASTRY:
60 g (2 oz) margarine
2/3 cup water
3/4 cup wholewheat flour
2 eggs
1/2 cup grated Cheddar
  cheese
FILLING:
2 tablespoons oil
1 onion, chopped
250 g (8 oz) mushrooms,
  sliced
2 cloves garlic, crushed
1 tablespoon wholewheat
  flour
2/3 cup vegetable stock
3/4 cup roughly chopped
  walnuts
2 tablespoons chopped
  parsley
salt and pepper

Melt the margarine in a large pan, add the water and bring to the boil. Add the flour all at once and beat until the mixture leaves the side of the pan. Cool slightly, then add the eggs one at a time, beating vigorously until glossy. Beat in the cheese. Spoon the pastry around the edge of a greased 6 cup ovenproof dish.

To make the filling, heat the oil in a pan, add the onion and fry until softened. Add the mushrooms and garlic and fry for 2 minutes. Stir in the flour, then add the stock and bring to the boil, stirring. Cook for 3 minutes, until thickened. Stir in all but 2 tablespoons of the walnuts, the parsley, and salt and pepper to taste.

Pour the filling into the centre of the dish and sprinkle with the reserved walnuts.

Bake in a preheated moderately hot oven, 200°C (400°F), for 40 to 45 minutes, until the pastry is golden brown. Serve immediately.
Serves 4

EGGPLANT GALETTE

2 large eggplant
salt and pepper
⅔ cup olive oil
1 onion, chopped
1 clove garlic, crushed
500 g (1 lb) tomatoes,
    skinned and chopped
1 egg
250 g (8 oz) Ricotta or
    cottage cheese
1 tablespoon sesame seeds,
    toasted

Slice the eggplant, sprinkle with salt and leave in a colander for 1 hour. Rinse well and dry on kitchen paper.

Heat 2 tablespoons oil in a pan, add the onion and fry until softened. Add the garlic and tomatoes and simmer, uncovered, for 5 to 7 minutes.

Mix the egg with the cheese, adding salt and pepper to taste.

Heat the remaining oil in a frying pan, add the eggplant and cook on both sides until golden. Drain on kitchen paper.

Arrange a layer of overlapping eggplant slices on the bottom and side of an 18 cm (7 inch) springform cake tin. Cover with half the tomato mixture, then top with half the cheese mixture. Repeat the layers, finishing with eggplant. Cover with foil and bake in a preheated moderate oven, 180°C (350°F), for 40 to 50 minutes.

Turn out onto a warmed serving dish and sprinkle with the sesame seeds. Cut into wedges and serve with crusty wholewheat bread.
Serves 4

CURRIED VEGBURGERS

2 tablespoons oil
2 onions, chopped
1 clove garlic, crushed
2 carrots, chopped
2 celery sticks, chopped
2 teaspoons curry powder
2 tablespoons chopped
    parsley
500 g (1 lb) potatoes,
    boiled and mashed
salt and pepper
wholewheat breadcrumbs
    for coating
oil for shallow-frying

Heat the oil in a pan, add the onions and fry until softened. Add the garlic, carrots and celery and fry for 5 minutes, stirring. Mix in the curry powder and cook for 1 minute.

Add the fried vegetables and parsley to the potato and season with salt and pepper to taste. Divide the mixture into 8 pieces, shape into rounds, and coat with breadcrumbs. Press to flatten slightly and fry for 2 minutes on each side until golden. Serve with Piquant Sauce (page 93).

Serves 4

SPINACH AND MUSHROOM PLAIT

3 tablespoons oil
1 onion, chopped
500 g (1 lb) frozen
    chopped spinach, half-
    thawed
pinch of grated nutmeg
salt and pepper
250 g (8 oz) button
    mushrooms, sliced
2 cloves garlic, crushed
wholemeal shortcrust
    pastry, made with
    3 cups flour (see
    Spinach Lattice Flan,
    page 42)
beaten egg to glaze
1 tablespoon sesame seeds

Heat 1 tablespoon oil in a pan, add the onion and fry until softened. Add the spinach, nutmeg, and salt and pepper to taste and cook for 5 minutes, stirring. Turn onto a plate to cool.

Wipe out the pan and heat the remaining oil. Add the mushrooms and garlic and fry until softened. Season to taste with salt and pepper; allow to cool.

Roll out the pastry on a floured surface to 30×35 cm (12×14 inches). Mark into 3 sections lengthways. Moisten the edges with water. Make diagonal slits along the outer sections of the pastry, 2.5 cm (1 inch) apart and 7.5 cm (3 inches) long.

Spread half the spinach mixture over the centre section of the dough, place the mushrooms on top, then cover with remaining spinach. Fold the cut pastry strips over the spinach to give a plaited effect. Press each end firmly to seal. Carefully lift onto a baking sheet and chill for 20 minutes.

Brush with egg and sprinkle with sesame seeds. Bake in a preheated moderately hot oven, 200°C (400°F), for 30 to 35 minutes, until golden brown. Serve with salad.

Serves 4 to 6

WALNUT-STUFFED EGGPLANT

2 large eggplant
2 tablespoons olive oil
1 large onion, chopped
2 cloves garlic, crushed
3 celery sticks, chopped
185 g (6 oz) mushrooms,
    chopped
6 tablespoons brown rice,
    cooked
½ cup finely chopped
    walnuts
1 tablespoon tomato paste
2 tablespoons chopped
    parsley
salt and pepper to taste
¾ cup grated Cheddar
    cheese

Prick the eggplant all over, cut in half
and place cut side down on a greased
baking sheet. Bake in a preheated
moderately hot oven, 190°C (375°F),
for 30 minutes.

Meanwhile, heat the oil in a pan,
add the onion and fry until softened.
Add the garlic and celery and fry for
5 minutes. Add the mushrooms and
cook, stirring, for 3 minutes. Stir in
rice, walnuts, tomato paste, parsley,
and seasoning. Turn off the heat.

Scoop the flesh from the eggplant,
without breaking the skins, chop
finely and mix with the fried mixture.
Pile into the eggplant skins, sprinkle
with the cheese and place under a
preheated hot grill until heated
through. Serve immediately.
Serves 4

VEGETABLE CURRY

2 tablespoons oil
1 onion, sliced
2 teaspoons ground
    coriander
2 teaspoons ground cumin
2 cloves garlic, crushed
2 tablespoons finely
    chopped root ginger
1 × 400 g can chopped
    tomatoes
2/3 cup water
1 green chilli, finely
    chopped
2 potatoes, diced
2 carrots, sliced
180 g (6 oz) okra,
    topped, tailed and cut
    into 2.5 cm (1 inch)
    lengths
250 g (8 oz) cauliflower,
    broken into florets
salt and pepper
2 tablespoons chopped
    fresh coriander

ACCOMPANIMENTS:
4 poppadums
DAHL:
2 tablespoons oil
1 onion, chopped
2 cloves garlic, chopped
2 teaspoons garam masala
1 teaspoon turmeric
1 cup red lentils
2½ cups water
1 tablespoon chopped
    coriander

CUCUMBER RAITA:
¼ cucumber
2/3 cup natural yogurt
paprika
ONION RELISH:
125 g (4 oz) white onion,
    thinly sliced
1 tablespoon lemon juice
¼ teaspoon paprika
pinch of cayenne pepper

Heat the oil in a large pan, add the onion and fry until softened. Add the ground coriander, cumin, garlic and ginger and fry for 1 minute, stirring constantly. Add the tomatoes, water, chilli, potatoes, carrots, okra, cauliflower and salt and pepper to taste. Mix to coat the vegetables with the sauce. Cover and cook gently for 20 minutes, until tender. Stir in the chopped coriander.

Serve on a bed of brown rice with the following accompaniments.

POPPADUMS
Fry in a deep hot oil for a few seconds until they have puffed up. Drain thoroughly on kitchen paper.

DAHL
Heat the oil in a pan, add the onion and fry until softened. Add the garlic and spices and fry for 1 minute. Add the remaining ingredients, bring to the boil and simmer for 20 minutes, stirring occasionally. Serve hot.

CUCUMBER RAITA
Grate the cucumber and drain off any juices. Mix with the yogurt, and salt to taste. Turn into a serving bowl and sprinkle with paprika.

ONION RELISH
Mix the onion with the lemon juice, peppers and salt to taste until well coated. Leave to stand for 1 hour, then turn into a serving dish and sprinkle with more paprika.

Serves 4

CHEESE AND EGG DISHES

SPINACH AND CHEESE SOUFFLÉ

30 g (1 oz) margarine
1/4 cup wholemeal flour
2/3 cup milk
3 eggs, separated
125 g (4 oz) frozen
   spinach purée, thawed
1/2 cup grated Cheddar
   cheese
1/4 teaspoon grated nutmeg
salt and pepper
2 tablespoons grated
   Parmesan cheese

Tie a double band of foil around a greased 5 cup soufflé dish, to come 5 cm (2 inches) above the rim.

Melt the margarine in a pan and stir in the flour. Remove from the heat and stir in the milk. Return to the heat and slowly bring to the boil, stirring. Cook for 3 minutes, then add the egg yolks, spinach, Cheddar cheese, nutmeg, and salt and pepper to taste. Mix thoroughly.

Whisk the egg whites until fairly stiff, then carefully fold into the spinach mixture using a metal spoon.

Turn into the prepared dish, sprinkle with the Parmesan cheese and cook in a preheated moderately hot oven, 190°C (375°F), for 30 to 35 minutes, until risen and golden. Serve immediately.
Serves 4

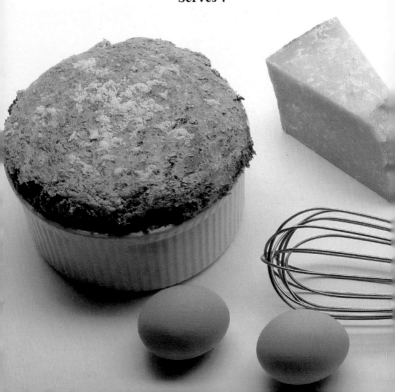

CHEESE AND VEGETABLE GRATIN

2 tablespoons oil
2 onions, sliced
1 clove garlic, crushed
375 g (12 oz) zucchini,
    sliced
1 tablespoon chopped
    parsley
1 teaspoon chopped thyme
salt and pepper
4 large tomatoes, skinned
    and sliced
30 g (1 oz) margarine
¼ cup wholemeal flour
1¼ cups milk
1 cup grated Cheddar
    cheese
1 tablespoon fresh
    wholewheat
    breadcrumbs

Heat the oil in a pan, add the onions and fry gently until softened. Add the garlic, zucchini, herbs, and salt and pepper to taste, and cook for 5 minutes, stirring occasionally.

Put half the mixture in a 6 cup pie dish and cover with the tomatoes. Top with remaining mixture.

Melt the margarine in a saucepan, stir in the flour, remove from the heat and blend in the milk. Bring to the boil, stirring constantly, until the sauce thickens. Add half of the cheese, and salt and pepper to taste and pour over the zucchini.

Sprinkle with the breadcrumbs, then the remaining cheese. Bake in a preheated moderate oven, 180°C (350°F), for 30 minutes, until golden.
Serves 4

BROCCOLI AND CHEESE FLAN

CHEESE PASTRY:
1 cup wholemeal flour
½ cup plain flour, sifted
90 g (3 oz) margarine
½ cup grated matured
   Cheddar cheese
½ teaspoon dried mixed
   herbs
1 egg yolk
iced water to mix
FILLING:
250 g (8 oz) broccoli
2 eggs, beaten
⅔ cup milk
1 cup grated Cheddar
   cheese
1 teaspoon dry mustard
salt and pepper

Place the flours in a bowl and rub in the margarine until the mixture resembles fine breadcrumbs. Stir in the cheese and herbs. Make a well in the centre and add the egg yolk and enough water to mix to a firm dough.

Turn onto a floured surface and knead lightly until smooth. Roll out and use to line a 20 cm (8 inch) flan dish. Prick the base with a fork; chill for 20 minutes. Bake 'blind' in a preheated moderately hot oven, 200°C (400°F), for 10 minutes. Remove the foil and beans, return to oven for 5 minutes.

Meanwhile, cook the broccoli in boiling salted water for 5 to 6 minutes. Rinse in cold water, drain thoroughly, then chop roughly.

Mix the beaten eggs with the milk, three quarters of the cheese, the mustard, and salt and pepper to taste.

Arrange the broccoli in the flan case and pour over the egg mixture. Sprinkle with remaining cheese and return to the oven for 35 minutes, until set and golden.
Serves 4

RICOTTA AND SPINACH PANCAKES

PANCAKE BATTER:
1 cup wholemeal flour
pinch of salt
1 egg, beaten
1¼ cups milk

FILLING:
375 g (12 oz) frozen chopped spinach, half thawed
185 g (6 oz) Ricotta or cottage cheese
2 tablespoons grated Parmesan cheese
1 egg
salt and pepper
grated nutmeg

SAUCE:
2 tablespoons oil
2 tablespoons flour
1¼ cups milk
½ cup grated Cheddar cheese

TO FINISH:
1 tablespoon grated Parmesan cheese
1 tablespoon wholewheat breadcrumbs

Make and cook the pancakes as for Provençale Pancakes (page 43).

Place the spinach in a pan and heat gently until completely thawed. Cook for 2 minutes, then pour off any liquid. Beat in the cheeses, egg, and salt, pepper and nutmeg to taste.

Divide the filling between the pancakes, roll up and place in an oiled shallow ovenproof dish.

To make the sauce, heat the oil in a pan, remove from the heat and stir in the flour. Stir in the milk until blended, return to the heat and bring to the boil, stirring, until thickened. Remove from the heat and stir in the cheese.

Spoon the sauce over the pancakes, then sprinkle with the Parmesan cheese and breadcrumbs. Cook in a preheated moderately hot oven, 190°C (375°F), for 15 to 20 minutes, until golden.
Serves 4

FRITTATA VERDE

375 g (12 oz) spinach
3 tablespoons oil
1 onion, chopped
6 eggs
2 tablespoons grated
   Parmesan cheese
1/2 teaspoon grated nutmeg
salt and pepper

Cook the spinach with just the water clinging to its leaves after washing, for 6 to 8 minutes. Drain well, squeeze dry, then chop finely.

Heat 1 tablespoon of the oil in a pan, add the onion and fry until softened. Mix with the spinach.

Break the eggs into a bowl, add the cheese, spinach mixture, nutmeg, and salt and pepper to taste.

Heat the remaining oil in a 23 cm (9 inch) frying pan, and the egg mixture and stir lightly until beginning to set. Cook for about 5 minutes, until the underneath is set, then invert a large plate over the pan, turn the pan over and ease the frittata onto the plate. Add a little more oil to the pan, heat it then slide the frittata back into the pan and cook until the other side is set.

Cut into wedges and serve with salad and wholewheat bread.
Serves 4

RATATOUILLE AU GRATIN

6 tablespoons olive oil
1 small eggplant, sliced
2 cloves garlic, crushed
375 g (12 oz) zucchini,
   sliced
1 red pepper, cored, seeded
   and sliced
375 g (12 oz) tomatoes,
   skinned and sliced
1 tablespoon chopped basil
salt and pepper
500 g (1 lb) potatoes,
   boiled and sliced
250 g (8 oz) Mozzarella
   cheese, thinly sliced

Heat half the oil in a frying pan, add the eggplant and fry on both sides until just beginning to brown, adding more oil if necessary. Remove from the pan and drain on kitchen paper.

Add the remaining oil to the pan and fry the garlic, zucchini and red pepper for 8 to 10 minutes, until softened, stirring occasionally. Add the tomatoes, basil, eggplant, and salt and pepper to taste and simmer for 10 minutes.

Place the potatoes in a shallow ovenproof dish and cover with the ratatouille. Spread evenly to the edges and arrange the cheese slices over the top. Bake in a preheated moderately hot oven, 190°C (375°F), for 15 to 20 minutes, until the cheese begins to melt. Serve immediately.
Serves 4

SPANISH OMELET

3 tablespoons olive oil
2 onions, chopped
2 cloves garlic, crushed
1 red pepper, cored, seeded
  and chopped
4 eggs
salt and pepper
2 large potatoes, boiled
  and chopped
2 tablespoons chopped
  parsley

Heat 2 tablespoons of the oil in a
25 cm (10 inch) frying pan, add the
onions and cook until softened. Add
the garlic and red pepper; cook for 8
to 10 minutes, stirring occasionally.

Whisk the eggs, with salt and
pepper to taste, in a bowl, then stir in
the potatoes, parsley and fried
vegetables.

Heat the remaining oil in the pan,
pour in the egg mixture and spread
evenly to the edge. Cook for about 5
minutes, shaking the pan to prevent
the omelet sticking, until it comes
away from the side of the pan.

Place the pan under a preheated
moderate grill for about 3 minutes to
cook the top. Slide the omelet onto a
warmed serving plate and cut into
wedges to serve.
Serves 4

ZUCCHINI ROULADE

30 g (1 oz) margarine
500 g (1 lb) zucchini,
    grated
4 eggs, separated
1 teaspoon chopped thyme
1 tablespoon chopped
    parsley
salt and pepper
2 tablespoons grated
    Parmesan cheese

FILLING:
2 tablespoons oil
1 onion, chopped
185 g (6 oz) mushrooms,
    sliced
1 tablespoon wholemeal
    flour
½ cup milk

Melt the margarine in a pan, add the zucchini and fry for 7 to 8 minutes, stirring frequently, until coloured.

Place in a bowl with the egg yolks, herbs, and salt and pepper to taste and mix well. Whisk the egg whites until fairly stiff, fold 2 tablespoons into the zucchini mixture to lighten it, then carefully fold in the rest.

Turn the mixture into a lined and greased 30 × 20 cm (12 × 8 inch) Swiss roll tin and spread evenly. Cook in a preheated moderately hot oven, 200°C (400°F), for 10 to 15 minutes, until risen and firm.

Meanwhile, prepare the filling. Heat the oil in a pan, add the onion and fry until softened. Add the mushrooms and fry for 3 minutes. Stir in the flour, then gradually stir in the milk. Add salt and pepper to taste and simmer for 3 minutes.

Sprinkle the Parmesan cheese on a sheet of greaseproof paper. Turn the roulade out onto the paper and peel off the lining paper. Spread with the filling and roll up like a Swiss roll. Serve immediately.
Serves 4

PROVENÇALE TARTLETS

wholemeal shortcrust
  pastry made with 2 cups
  flour (see Spinach
  Lattice Flan, page 42)
tablespoon olive oil
onion, chopped
clove garlic, crushed
red pepper, cored, seeded
  and sliced
185 g (6 oz) zucchini,
  thinly sliced
4 tomatoes, skinned and
  chopped
1 tablespoon chopped
  marjoram
1 tablespoon chopped basil
salt and pepper
1 egg
1/3 cup cream
1/2 cup grated Gruyère
  cheese

Roll out the pastry on a lightly
floured surface and use to line six
11 cm (4½ inch) individual flan tins.
Prick the base of each and chill for
20 minutes.

Bake 'blind' in a preheated
moderately hot oven, 200°C (400°F),
for 10 minutes. Remove the foil and
beans.

Heat the oil in a pan, add the onion
and fry until softened. Add the garlic,
remaining vegetables, herbs, and salt
and pepper to taste, cover and
simmer for 15 minutes, then spoon
into the pastry cases.

Beat the egg, cream and cheese
together, seasoning with a little salt
and pepper, and pour over the filling.
Lower the oven temperature to 190°C
(375°F), and cook the tartlets for 15 to
20 minutes, until set.

Makes 6

PULSES, BEANS AND NUTS

LENTIL AND TOMATO QUICHE

cheese pastry made with
   1½ cups flour (see
   Broccoli and Cheese
   Flan, page 55)
2 tablespoons oil
2 onions, chopped
2 celery sticks, chopped
1 clove garlic, crushed
1 cup green lentils
1 × 400 g can chopped
   tomatoes
1 cup water
salt and pepper
3 tablespoons chopped
   parsley
¾ cup grated Cheddar
   cheese
1 tablespoon sesame seeds

Roll out the pastry on a lightly
floured surface and use to line a 20 cm
(8 inch) flan dish. Prick the base with
a fork and chill for 20 minutes.

Bake 'blind' in a preheated
moderately hot oven, 200°C (400°F),
for 10 to 12 minutes. Remove the foil
and beans and return to the oven for
5 minutes.

Meanwhile, heat the oil in a pan,
add the onions, celery and garlic and
fry until softened. Add the lentils,
tomatoes with their juice, water, and
salt and pepper to taste. Cover and
simmer for 1 hour, stirring
occasionally, until the lentils are
tender. Stir in the parsley and turn
into the flan case. Sprinkle with the
cheese and sesame seeds and return to
the oven for 10 to 15 minutes, until
the cheese is brown and bubbling.
Serves 4

LENTIL AND MUSHROOM AU GRATIN

tablespoons oil
onion, chopped
carrot, chopped
celery sticks, chopped
clove garlic, crushed
1/4 cups red lentils
2 1/2 cups water
tablespoons shoyu *
salt and pepper
MUSHROOM FILLING:
30 g (1 oz) margarine
250 g (8 oz) flat
    mushrooms, sliced
2 cloves garlic, crushed
3 tablespoons chopped
    parsley
TO FINISH:
3/4 cup grated Cheddar
    cheese

Heat the oil in a pan, add the onion, carrot and celery and fry gently for 10 minutes, until softened. Add the remaining ingredients, with salt and pepper to taste. Cover and simmer for 50 minutes to 1 hour, stirring occasionally, until the lentils are tender.

Meanwhile, prepare the filling. Melt the margarine in a frying pan, add the mushrooms and fry for 2 minutes, stirring. Add the garlic, parsley, and salt and pepper to taste and mix well.

Place half the lentil mixture in an oiled shallow ovenproof dish. Spread the mushrooms over the top, then cover with the remaining lentil mixture. Top with the cheese and bake in a preheated moderately hot oven, 190°C (375°F), for 20 to 25 minutes until golden and bubbling.

Serve with salad and crusty bread.
Serves 4

CHEESE AND LENTIL GRATIN

1 tablespoon oil
1 onion, chopped
1 carrot, chopped
1 celery stick, chopped
1 cup red lentils
2 cups water
1 clove garlic, crushed
salt and pepper
2 tablespoons fresh
   wholewheat
   breadcrumbs
1 cup grated Cheddar
   cheese
2 tablespoons chopped
   parsley
1 egg, beaten
2 tablespoons sesame seeds
parsley sprigs to garnish
   (optional)

Heat the oil in a pan, add the onion and fry until softened. Add the carrot, celery, lentils, water, garlic, and salt and pepper to taste. Cover, bring to the boil, then lower the heat and simmer gently for about 20 minutes, until all the water is absorbed.

Add three quarters of the cheese, the parsley and egg to the lentil mixture. Stir until thoroughly mixed. Spoon the mixture into a 4 cup shallow ovenproof dish and smooth the top.

Sprinkle the sesame seeds and remaining cheese over the top. Bake in a preheated moderate oven, 180°C (350°F), for 45 minutes, until the topping is crisp and golden brown.

Garnish with parsley and serve hot with Tomato Sauce (see page 93), new potatoes and a seasonal green vegetable.

This tasty gratin is also excellent served cold with a crisp green salad.
Serves 6

LENTIL MOUSSAKA

²⁄₃ cup oil
1 onion, chopped
4 celery sticks, chopped
1 clove garlic, crushed
1 × 400 g can tomatoes
1¼ cups green lentils
2 tablespoons shoyu*
¼ teaspoon pepper
4 cups water
500 g (1 lb) eggplant
salt
TOPPING:
2 eggs, beaten
²⁄₃ cup yogurt
TO FINISH:
2 tablespoons grated
    Parmesan cheese

Heat 1 tablespoon of the oil in a pan, add the onion and cook until softened. Add the celery, garlic, tomatoes with their juice, lentils, shoyu, pepper and water. Cover and simmer for 50 minutes, until cooked.

Meanwhile, slice the eggplant, sprinkle with salt and leave in a colander for 1 hour. Drain and pat dry with kitchen paper.

Heat some of the remaining oil in a frying pan, add the eggplant in batches and cook on both sides until golden; add more oil as required. Drain on kitchen paper.

Cover the base of a shallow ovenproof dish with the lentil mixture and arrange a layer of eggplant slices on top. Repeat the layers, finishing with eggplant.

Mix the topping ingredients with salt and pepper to taste, and pour over the eggplant. Top with the cheese and bake in a preheated moderate oven, 180°C (350°F), for 30 to 40 minutes, until golden.
Serves 4

PROVENÇALE BEAN STEW

2 cups haricot beans or
    pinto beans, soaked
    overnight
salt and pepper
2 tablespoons olive oil
2 onions, sliced
1 red pepper, cored, seeded
    and sliced
1 green pepper, cored,
    seeded and sliced
2 cloves garlic, crushed
1 × 400 g can chopped
    tomatoes
2 tablespoons tomato paste
1 teaspoon chopped
    marjoram
1 bouquet garni
1/3 cup black olives,
    halved and stoned
2 tablespoons chopped
    parsley

Drain the beans, place in a pan and
cover with cold water. Bring to the
boil, boil rapidly for 10 minutes, then
cover and simmer for 1 to 1¼ hours,
until almost tender, adding a pinch of
salt towards the end of cooking.
Drain, reserving 1¼ cups of the
liquid.

Heat the oil in a pan, add the
onions and fry until softened. Add
the peppers and garlic and fry gently
for 10 minutes. Add the tomatoes
with their juice, tomato paste, herbs,
beans, reserved liquid, and salt and
pepper to taste. Cover and simmer
for 45 minutes, adding the olives and
parsley 5 minutes before the end of
the cooking time. Remove the
bouquet garni.

Serve with garlic bread and salad.
Serves 4

FASOLIA

Fasolia is widely eaten in Greece. It is usually served as a vegetable dish, either hot or cold, but with the addition of more water and further seasoning, if necessary, it can also be served as a soup.

4 tablespoons olive oil
1 large onion, chopped
1 clove garlic, crushed
1¼ cups haricot beans,
    soaked overnight
1 bouquet garni
1 tablespoon tomato paste
4 tomatoes, skinned and
    chopped
2½ cups water
salt and pepper
2 teaspoons lemon juice
TO FINISH:
thinly sliced onion rings
coarsely chopped parsley

Heat the oil in a pan, add the onion and fry until pale golden. Add the garlic, drained beans, bouquet garni, tomato paste and tomatoes, then pour over the water. Bring to the boil, boil for 10 minutes, then cover and simmer for 1¾ hours or until the beans are tender, adding salt and pepper to taste towards the end of the cooking time; the liquid should be the consistency of a thick sauce. Remove the bouquet garni.

Add the lemon juice, check the seasoning and turn into a warmed serving dish. Garnish with the onion rings and parsley.
Serves 4

TANDOORI CUTLETS

1¼ cups black-eyed
   beans, soaked overnight
2 cloves garlic, crushed
1 tablespoon shoyu*
2 teaspoons tandoori spice
   mixture
2 tablespoons chopped
   coriander
8 spring onions, chopped
2 carrots, grated
salt and pepper
oil for shallow-frying
COATING:
1 teaspoon tandoori spice
   mixture
1 cup wholewheat
   breadcrumbs

Drain the beans, place in a pan and cover with cold water. Bring to the boil, boil rapidly for 10 minutes, then cover and simmer for 20 to 25 minutes, until tender. Drain well, then mash.

Add the remaining ingredients, with salt and pepper to taste, and mix well.

Shape into 8 ovals and flatten to about 1 cm (½ inch) thick. Mix the tandoori spice mixture with the breadcrumbs and use to coat the cutlets completely. Fry in hot shallow oil for 4 minutes on each side. Serve hot.
Serves 4

MIXED BEAN CASSEROLE

1 cup red kidney beans,
   soaked overnight
1 cup butter beans, soaked
   overnight
2 tablespoons oil
2 onions, sliced
2 celery sticks, sliced
2 carrots, sliced
2 cloves garlic, crushed
1 tablespoon wholemeal
   flour
1 × 400 g can chopped
   tomatoes
1 tablespoon tomato paste
1 bouquet garni
salt and pepper
TOPPING:
1 small wholewheat
   French stick
60 g (2 oz) margarine
1 clove garlic, crushed
1 tablespoon chopped
   parsley
1 tablespoon sesame seeds

Drain the beans, place in separate pans and cover with cold water. Bring to the boil, boil rapidly for 10 minutes, then cover and simmer for 1 hour, or until tender. Drain, reserving ⅔ cup of the liquid.

Heat oil in a flameproof casserole, add the onions and fry until softened. Add celery, carrots and garlic and fry for 3 to 4 minutes. Stir in the flour. Add remaining ingredients, with the beans, reserved liquid, salt and pepper to taste. Cover and cook in a pre-heated moderate oven, 180°C (350°F), for 1 hour. Discard bouquet garni. Increase the temperature to 200°C (400°F).

Meanwhile, prepare the topping. Cut the French stick into 1 cm (½ inch) diagonal slices. Mix together the margarine, garlic, parsley, and salt and pepper to taste and spread on one side of each piece of bread.

Arrange plain side down to cover the top of the casserole. Sprinkle with the sesame seeds and return to the oven for 20 minutes.
Serves 4

BLACK BEAN CURRY

2½ cups black beans, soaked overnight
salt
3 tablespoons oil
2 onions, sliced
2 teaspoons ground cumin
2 teaspoons ground coriander
1 teaspoon garam masala
1 teaspoon chilli powder
1 cm (½ inch) piece root ginger, peeled and finely chopped
4 cloves garlic, crushed
1 × 400 g can tomatoes
3 celery sticks, sliced
1 teaspoon cardamom seeds
1 tablespoon chopped coriander

Drain the beans, place in a pan and cover with cold water. Bring to the boil, boil rapidly for 10 minutes, then cover and simmer for 1½ hours, until almost tender, adding a pinch of salt towards the end of the cooking time. Drain, reserving 1¼ cups of the liquid.

Heat the oil in a pan, add the onions and fry until softened. Add the cumin, ground coriander, garam masala, chilli powder, ginger and garlic and fry for 1 minute, stirring constantly. Add the reserved liquid, beans, tomatoes with their juice, celery, cardamom seeds, and salt to taste. Cover and simmer for 45 minutes, then stir in the chopped coriander. Serve with brown rice and Cucumber Raita (see page 50).
Serves 4–6

WALNUT AND LENTIL LOAF

1 tablespoon oil
1 onion, chopped
1 clove garlic, crushed
2 celery sticks, sliced
1 cup green lentils
2 cups water
125 g (4 oz) walnuts,
    finely chopped
1 cup wholewheat
    breadcrumbs
2 tablespoons chopped
    parsley
1 tablespoon shoyu*
1 egg, beaten
salt and pepper
thyme sprigs to garnish

Heat the oil in a pan, add the onion and fry until softened. Add the garlic, celery, lentils and water and bring to the boil. Cover and simmer gently for 50 to 60 minutes, until the lentils are tender, stirring occasionally and removing the lid for the last 10 minutes to allow the moisture to evaporate.

Mix in the walnuts, breadcrumbs, parsley, shoyu, egg, and salt and pepper to taste, and mix thoroughly.

Line a 5 cup loaf tin with foil to cover the bottom and long sides. Brush with oil. Spoon the mixture into the tin, cover with foil and bake in a preheated moderately hot oven, 190°C (375°F), for 45 to 50 minutes.

Leave in the tin for 2 minutes, then loosen with a knife and turn out onto a warmed serving dish. Garnish with thyme and serve with Piquant Sauce (see page 93).
Serves 6

HAZELNUT AND VEGETABLE LOAF

2 tablespoons oil
1 onion, chopped
1 clove garlic, crushed
2 celery sticks, chopped
1 tablespoon wholemeal
    flour
¾ cup tomato juice
125 g (4 oz) hazelnuts,
    ground and browned
2 cups wholewheat
    breadcrumbs
2 carrots, grated
1 tablespoon shoyu*
2 tablespoons chopped
    parsley
1 egg, beaten
salt and pepper

Heat the oil in a pan, add the onion and fry until softened. Add the garlic and celery and fry for 5 minutes, stirring occasionally. Mix in the flour, then stir in the tomato juice until thickened.

Place the remaining ingredients, with salt and pepper to taste, in a bowl and add the tomato mixture, stirring until blended.

Turn into a lined and greased 5 cup loaf tin, cover with foil and bake in a preheated moderate oven, 180°C (350°F), for 1 hour.

Turn out onto a warmed serving dish and serve hot with Tomato Sauce (see page 93), or cold with a mixed salad.
Serves 4

PEANUT AND MUSHROOM ROAST

3 tablespoons oil
1 onion, chopped
2 celery sticks, chopped
2 cloves garlic, crushed
250 g (8 oz) peanuts,
    ground
2 cups wholewheat
    breadcrumbs
250 g (8 oz) potato,
    boiled and mashed
1 egg, beaten
1 tablespoon shoyu*
1 tablespoon tomato paste
2 tablespoons chopped
    parsley
salt and pepper
250 g (8 oz) mushrooms,
    sliced
coriander leaves to garnish

Heat 1 tablespoon of the oil in a pan, add the onion, celery and garlic and fry until softened.

Mix the peanuts and breadcrumbs together in a bowl. Add the fried vegetables, potato, egg, shoyu, tomato paste, parsley, and salt and pepper to taste and mix thoroughly.

Heat the remaining oil in a pan, add the mushrooms and fry for 2 minutes, stirring.

Grease an 8 cup loaf tin and press in half the nut mixture. Cover with the mushrooms, then press the remaining nut mixture on top.

Cover with foil and bake in a pre-heated moderate oven, 180°C (350°F), for about 1 hour.

Leave in the tin for 5 minutes, then turn out onto a warmed serving dish. Garnish with coriander and serve with Mushroom Sauce (see page 93).
Serves 4 to 6

NUT CROQUETTES

1 tablespoon oil
1 onion, chopped
1 celery stick, chopped
1 clove garlic, crushed
90 g (3 oz) mushrooms,
    chopped
2 teaspoons ground
    coriander
2 tablespoons plain flour
2/3 cup water
1 tablespoon shoyu*
125 g (4 oz) cashew nuts,
    ground
2 cups wholewheat
    breadcrumbs
2 tablespoons chopped
    parsley
salt and pepper
wholemeal flour to coat
oil for shallow-frying

Heat the oil in a pan, add the onion
and fry until softened. Add the
celery, garlic and mushrooms and fry
for 5 minutes, stirring occasionally.
Add the coriander and fry for
1 minute, then stir in the flour.
Remove from the heat and stir in the
water and shoyu until thickened. Add
the cashew nuts, breadcrumbs and
parsley, and salt and pepper to taste
and mix well. Divide the mixture
into 8 pieces, using dampened hands,
then shape into croquettes.

   Place the flour in a plastic bag, add
the croquettes one at a time and shake
until well coated. Fry in hot shallow
oil for 2 minutes on each side, until
golden brown and crisp. Serve with
Tomato Sauce (see page 93).
Serves 4

71

DESSERTS

KIWI AND GINGER SALAD

1 honeydew melon,
    halved and seeded
2 kiwi fruit, thinly sliced
250 g (8 oz) green grapes,
    halved and pipped
15 g (½ oz) stem ginger,
    thinly sliced
2 tablespoons ginger syrup
    (from the ginger)
4 tablespoons apple juice

Scoop the flesh from the melon halves with a melon baller, or cut into cubes, and place in a bowl with the kiwi fruit, grapes and ginger.

Mix the ginger syrup and apple juice together and pour over the fruit. Serve in individual dishes.

Serves 4–6

APPLE AND GRANOLA CRUNCH

500 g (1 lb) eating apples,
  peeled, cored and
  chopped
1½ cups chopped dates
1¼ cups apple juice
½ teaspoon ground
  cinnamon
½ cup cream, whipped
90 g (3 oz) Granola (see
  page 86)

Place the apples, dates, apple juice
and cinnamon in a pan, cover and
cook for 10 to 15 minutes, until the
apples are soft. Mash with a fork,
replace the lid and leave to cool.

Spoon half the mixture into 4 glass
serving dishes, top each with half the
cream, then sprinkle with three
quarters of the granola. Repeat the
layers, finishing with the remaining
granola.

Serves 4

STRAWBERRY CHEESE WITH ALMOND FINGERS

ALMOND FINGERS:
125 g (4 oz) margarine
1/3 cup brown sugar
1 cup wholemeal flour
1/4 cup ground almonds,
   toasted
1/4 cup blanched almonds,
   chopped

STRAWBERRY CHEESE:
2 tablespoons clear honey
185 g (6 oz) strawberries
185 g (6 oz) cottage
   cheese

Cream the margarine and sugar together until light and fluffy. Add the flour and ground almonds and stir until the mixture binds together.

Roll out the dough to an oblong and press into an 18 × 28 cm (7 × 11 inch) baking tin. Flatten with a palette knife and prick with a fork, then sprinkle with the chopped almonds and press in lightly. Bake in a preheated moderate oven, 180°C (350°F), for 30 to 35 minutes until pale golden. Allow to cool slightly, then mark into 20 fingers. Cool completely before removing from the tin.

Place the honey and half of the strawberries in an electric blender or food processor and work to a purée. Beat the cheese until smooth, then fold in the fruit purée. Slice the remaining strawberries, set aside 4 slices for decoration and divide the rest between individual dishes.

Spoon the strawberry cheese into the dishes, decorate with the reserved strawberry slices and serve with the almond fingers.

Serves 4

NOTE: Store any leftover almond fingers in an airtight tin.

HIGHLAND CREAM

1/4 cup blanched almonds,
   chopped
1/4 cup medium oatmeal
1/2 cup wholewheat
   breadcrumbs
1/2 cup cream
3 tablespoons whisky
2 tablespoons clear honey
2/3 cup natural yogurt

Mix together the almonds, oatmeal and breadcrumbs and place on a baking tray. Place under a preheated hot grill until golden brown, stirring frequently. Leave to cool.

Whip the cream, whisky and honey together until soft peaks form, then fold in the yogurt and the almond mixture. Spoon into individual glasses and chill until required.

Serves 6

BANANA AND APRICOT YOGURT

1 cup chopped dried
    apricots
300 g natural yogurt
1 banana
1 tablespoon flaked
    almonds, toasted

Place the apricots in a bowl with the
yogurt. Mix well, then cover and
leave in the refrigerator overnight.

Slice the banana and fold into the
yogurt mixture. Spoon into
individual glasses and sprinkle with
the almonds to serve.
Serves 4

FRUIT AND NUT CRUMBLE

185 g (6 oz) dried apricots
125 g (4 oz) dried pitted
  prunes
125 g (4 oz) dried figs
60 g (2 oz) dried apples
2½ cups apple juice
1½ cups wholemeal flour
90 g (3 oz) margarine
⅓ cup dark brown sugar
¼ cup hazelnuts, chopped

Place the dried fruits in a bowl with the apple juice and leave overnight. Transfer to a saucepan and simmer for 10 to 15 minutes, until softened. Turn into an ovenproof dish.

Place the flour in a bowl and rub in the margarine until the mixture resembles breadcrumbs. Stir in the sugar and hazelnuts, then sprinkle over the fruit.

Bake in a preheated moderately hot oven, 200°C (400°F), for 25 to 30 minutes. Serve with Yogurt Snow (see page 80).

Serves 6-8

Variation: For the topping, replace the hazelnuts with toasted chopped almonds or grated coconut.

APRICOT PANCAKES

PANCAKE BATTER:
½ cup buckwheat flour*
½ cup plain flour
1 egg, beaten
1¼ cups milk
1 tablespoon oil
FILLING:
*375 g (12 oz) dried
    apricots, chopped and
    soaked for 2 hours*
2 cups apple juice
TO FINISH:
2 tablespoons clear honey
*¼ cup flaked almonds,
    toasted*

Place the flours in a bowl and make a well in the centre. Add the egg, then gradually stir in half the milk and the oil. Beat thoroughly until smooth, then add the remaining milk.

Heat a 15 cm (6 inch) omelet pan and add 1 teaspoon oil. Pour in 1 tablespoon of the batter, tilting the pan to coat the bottom evenly. Cook until the underside is brown, then turn and cook for 10 seconds. Repeat with the remaining batter, stacking the pancakes as they are cooked.

To make the filling, place the apricots and apple juice in a pan, cover and cook gently for 10 minutes.

Place a little of the filling on each pancake, roll up and arrange in an ovenproof dish. Warm the honey and spoon over the pancakes to glaze. Bake in a preheated moderate oven, 180°C (350°F), for 10 to 15 minutes, until heated through. Sprinkle with the almonds and serve with Yogurt Snow (see page 80).
Serves 4

APPLE AND RAISIN PIE

1½ cups wholemeal flour
1 cup plain flour, sifted
150 g (5 oz) margarine
3-4 tablespoons iced water
FILLING:
750 g (1½ lb) eating
    apples, peeled, cored
    and thinly sliced
2 tablespoons brown sugar
1 teaspoon ground
    cinnamon
4 cloves
½ cup raisins
TO FINISH:
1 tablespoon sesame seeds

Place the flours in a bowl and rub in the margarine until the mixture resembles fine breadcrumbs. Stir in enough water to mix to a fairly stiff dough.

Turn onto a floured surface, knead lightly until smooth, then divide in half. Roll out one piece thinly and use to line a shallow 20 cm (8 inch) pie plate.

Layer the apples with the sugar, spices and raisins in the pastry case. Brush the pastry rim with cold water.

Roll out the remaining pastry and use to cover the pie. Seal and pinch the edges well, then trim off any surplus pastry with a sharp knife. Make a hole in the centre of the pie and chill for 20 minutes.

Brush with water and sprinkle with the sesame seeds. Bake in a preheated moderately hot oven, 200°C (400°F), for 30 to 40 minutes, until golden. Serve warm or cold with Yogurt Snow (see page 80).
Serves 6

DATE AND APPLE SHORTCAKE

NUT PASTRY:
90 g (3 oz) margarine
¼ cup brown sugar
1 cup wholemeal flour
*90 g (3 oz) brazil nuts,
    ground*
egg white for brushing
*1 tablespoon chopped
    brazil nuts*

FILLING:
3 tablespoons apple juice
*500 g (1 lb) eating apples,
    peeled and cored*
*125 g (4 oz) dates,
    chopped*
*1 teaspoon ground
    cinnamon*
½ cup cream, whipped

Beat the margarine and sugar together until softened. Stir in the flour and ground nuts and mix to a firm dough. Turn onto a floured surface; knead lightly until smooth. Divide in half and roll each piece into a 20 cm (8 inch) round on a baking sheet. Brush one with egg white and sprinkle with the chopped nuts.

Bake in a preheated moderately hot oven, 190°C (375°F), for 10 to 15 minutes, until golden. Cut the nut–covered round into 8 sections while warm. Transfer both rounds to a wire rack to cool.

Place the apple juice in a pan and slice the apples into it. Cover and cook gently for about 10 minutes, stirring occasionally, until just soft. Add the dates and cinnamon, cover and leave to cool.

Spread the apple filling over the whole shortcake round, cover with the cream, then arrange the cut triangles on top.
Serves 8

YOGURT SNOW

2 egg whites
3 tablespoons clear honey
300 g natural yogurt

Whisk the egg whites until stiff, then whisk in the honey and continue whisking until very thick. Carefully fold in the yogurt and serve immediately, instead of cream.
Makes about 2 cups

SUMMER PUDDING

500 g (1 lb) mixed
   blackberrries and
   blackcurrants
3 tablespoons clear honey
125 g (4 oz) raspberries
125 g (4 oz) strawberries
8 slices wholewheat bread,
   crusts removed

Place the blackberries, blackcurrants and honey in a heavy-based pan and cook gently for 10 to 15 minutes until tender, stirring occasionally. Add the raspberries and strawberries and leave to cool. Strain the fruit, reserving the juice.

Cut 3 circles of bread to fit the base, middle and top of a 4 cup pudding basin. Shape the remaining bread to fit round the side of the basin. Soak all the bread in the reserved fruit juice.

Line the bottom of the basin with the smallest circle of bread, then arrange the shaped bread around the side. Pour in half the fruit and place the middle sized circle of bread on top. Cover with the remaining fruit, then top with the largest bread circle. Fold over any bread protruding from the basin.

Cover with a saucer small enough to fit inside the basin and put a 500 g (1 lb) weight on top. Leave in the refrigerator overnight.

Turn onto a serving plate, pour over any remaining fruit juice and serve with whipped cream or Yogurt Snow (above).
Serves 8

NUT CREAM

125 g (4 oz) cashew nuts
²/₃ cup milk

Place the nuts and milk in an electric blender and blend until smooth. Chill and serve instead of cream.
Makes about ²/₃ cup

BAKING

CASHEW FLAPJACKS

125 g (4 oz) margarine
¼ cup clear honey
1 tablespoon malt extract
2¾ cups rolled oats
60 g (2 oz) cashew nuts,
    chopped

Place the margarine, honey and malt extract in a pan and heat gently until melted. Remove from the heat, stir in the rolled oats and cashew nuts and mix thoroughly. Turn into a greased shallow 18 × 28 cm (7 × 11 inch) tin and smooth the top with a palette knife.

Bake in a preheated moderate oven, 180°C (350°F), for 25 to 30 minutes.

Cool in the tin for 2 minutes, then cut into fingers. Allow to cool completely before removing the flapjacks from the tin.

Makes 20

MUESLI BISCUITS

125 g (4 oz) butter or margarine
¼ cup clear honey
3¼ cups muesli
2 tablespoons sunflower seeds

Place the butter or margarine and honey in a large pan and heat gently until melted. Remove from the heat, stir in the muesli and sunflower seeds and mix thoroughly.

Spoon mounds of the mixture onto lightly greased baking trays, spacing them well apart and flatten with a palette knife.

Bake in a preheated moderately hot oven, 190°C (375°F), for 10 to 12 minutes until golden brown. Leave for 3 minutes, then loosen the biscuits with a palette knife and leave on the baking trays until completely cool.

Makes 16

NOTE: The sweetness of these delicious biscuits will depend on the type of muesli used. If you use an unsweetened variety, add 1 to 2 tablespoons raw sugar, according to taste.

APRICOT AND NUT TEABREAD

2 cups All-Bran
1/3 cup raw sugar
3/4 cup dried apricots,
    snipped
1 1/4 cups apple juice
1 cup wholemeal flour
2 teaspoons baking
    powder, sifted
1/2 cup chopped hazelnuts

Place the All–Bran, sugar, apricots
and apple juice in a mixing bowl and
leave to soak for 1 hour.

Stir the flour, baking powder and
all but 1 tablespoon of the chopped
hazelnuts into the apricot mixture and
beat thoroughly.

Turn into a lined and greased 5 cup
loaf tin. Sprinkle the remaining nuts
over the top and bake in a preheated
moderate oven, 180°C (350°F), for
55 to 60 minutes.

Turn onto a wire rack to cool. Cut
into slices to serve.

Makes one 500 g (1 lb) loaf

FIGGY PRUNE CAKE

125 g (4 oz) pitted
    prunes, chopped
125 g (4 oz) dried figs,
    chopped
²/₃ cup apple juice
¼ cup clear honey
½ cup maize oil
2 eggs, beaten
1¼ cups wholemeal flour
½ teaspoon bicarbonate of
    soda
1 teaspoon ground mixed
    spice
½ teaspoon ground nutmeg
½ cup natural yogurt
¼ cup chopped walnuts

Place the prunes and figs in a pan with the apple juice, cover and simmer gently for 10 minutes. Leave to cool. Stir in the remaining ingredients, except the walnuts, and mix thoroughly.

Pour into a lined and greased deep 20 cm (8 inch) cake tin and sprinkle the walnuts over the top. Bake in a preheated moderate oven, 180°C (350°F), for 50 to 55 minutes, until firm to the touch. Leave in the tin for 2 minutes, then turn onto a wire rack to cool.

Makes one 20 cm (8 inch) cake

GRANOLA

1/2 cup safflower oil
1/3 cup malt extract
1/3 cup clear honey
1 1/2 cups rolled oats
2 cups toasted oat flakes
1 cup chopped hazelnuts
1/2 cup desiccated coconut
1/2 cup sunflower seeds
1/4 cup sesame seeds

Place the oil, malt and honey in a large pan and heat gently until the malt is runny. Mix in the remaining ingredients and stir thoroughly.

Turn into a large roasting pan and bake in a preheated moderately hot oven, 190°C (375°F), for 30 to 35 minutes, stirring occasionally. Leave to cool, then separate the pieces with your fingers.

Store in an airtight container. Serve with natural yogurt at breakfast time, or use as a topping for stewed fruits.
Makes 1 kg (2 lb)

GRANARY LOAF

2 cups granary or mixed
    grain flour
2 cups wholemeal flour
1 teaspoon salt
15 g (1/2 oz) fresh yeast
1 1/4 cups warm water
1 tablespoon malt extract
1 tablespoon oil
cracked wheat for
    sprinkling

Mix the flours and salt together in a bowl. Cream the yeast with a little of the water and leave until frothy. Add to the flour with the remaining water, malt and oil and mix to a dough.

Turn onto a floured surface. Knead for 5 minutes, until smooth and elastic. Place in a clean bowl, cover with a damp cloth and leave to rise in a warm place until doubled in size.

Turn onto a floured surface and knead for a few minutes. Shape into an 18 cm (7 inch) round and flatten slightly. Place on a greased baking sheet. Brush with water and sprinkle with cracked wheat. Cover and leave to rise in a warm place for about 30 minutes, until almost doubled in size.

Bake in a preheated hot oven, 220°C (425°F), for 25 to 30 minutes or until the bread sounds hollow when tapped underneath. Cool on a wire rack.
Makes 1 granary loaf

Granary Rolls: Divide the risen dough into 10 equal pieces. Knead each piece into a round and place on a floured baking sheet. Cover and leave to rise until doubled in size. Bake as above for 10 to 15 minutes.

WHOLEMEAL BREAD

12 cups wholemeal flour
3 teaspoons salt
30 g (1 oz) fresh yeast
4-5 cups warm water
2 tablespoons malt extract
2 tablespoons oil
1 tablespoon sesame seeds

Mix the flour and salt together in a bowl. Mix the yeast with a little of the water and leave until frothy. Add to the flour with the remaining water, malt extract and oil. Mix to a dough.

Turn onto a floured surface and knead for 8 to 10 minutes, until smooth and elastic. Place in a clean bowl, cover with a damp cloth and leave to rise in a warm place for about 2 hours, until doubled in size.

Turn onto a floured surface, knead for a few minutes, then divide into 2 pieces. Shape and place in greased 1 kg (2 lb) loaf tins. Brush with water and sprinkle with the sesame seeds.

Cover and leave to rise in a warm place for about 30 minutes, until the dough just reaches the top of the tins. Bake in a preheated hot oven, 220°C (425°F), for 15 minutes, then lower the temperature to 190°C (375°F), and bake for a further 20 to 25 minutes, until the bread sounds hollow when tapped underneath. Turn onto a wire rack to cool.

Makes two 1 kg (2 lb) loaves

Wholemeal Baps: Use ½ quantity dough, replacing half the water with warm milk. Divide the risen dough into 12 equal pieces. Knead each piece into a ball, then roll into a 10 cm (4 inch) round and place on floured baking sheets. Sprinkle with sesame seeds or flour. Cover and leave to rise until doubled in size. Bake in a preheated hot oven, 220°C (425°F), for 10 to 15 minutes. Cool on a wire rack.

SESAME THINS

1½ cups wholemeal flour
½ cup medium oatmeal
pinch of salt
1 teaspoon baking powder
90 g (3 oz) margarine
1 tablespoon malt extract
2 tablespoons milk
¼ cup sesame seeds

Place the flour, oatmeal and salt in a mixing bowl and sift in the baking powder; mix well. Rub in the margarine until the mixture resembles breadcrumbs.

Whisk the malt and milk together until blended, then add to the dry ingredients with the sesame seeds. Mix to a firm dough.

Turn onto a floured surface and roll out thinly. Cut into 6 cm (2½ inch) rounds with a plain cutter.

Place on a baking sheet and bake in a preheated moderately hot oven, 190°C (375°F), for 12 to 15 minutes, until golden. Transfer to a wire rack to cool. Serve with cheese.
Makes 20 to 24

LIGHT RYE BREAD

2 cups rye flour
4 cups wholemeal flour
2 teaspoons fine sea salt
15 g (½ oz) fresh yeast
2 cups warm water
2 tablespoons molasses or
    treacle
2 tablespoons oil
milk for brushing
1 teaspoon caraway seeds

Mix the flours and salt together in a bowl. Cream the yeast with a little of the water and leave until frothy. Add to the flour mixture with the remaining water, molasses and oil and mix thoroughly to a soft dough.

Turn onto a floured surface and knead for 5 minutes, until smooth and elastic. Place in a clean bowl, cover with a damp cloth and leave to rise in a warm place for about 2 hours, until doubled in size.

Turn onto a floured surface and knead for a few minutes. Shape into 2 oval loaves and place on greased baking trays. Prick with a fork in 8 or 9 places, then leave to rise in a warm place for 30 minutes, until doubled in size.

Brush with milk, sprinkle with the caraway seeds and bake in a preheated hot oven, 220°C (425°F), for 10 minutes. Lower the heat to 190°C (375°F), and bake for a further 25 to 30 minutes, until the loaves sound hollow when tapped underneath. Cool on a wire rack.

Makes 2 loaves

Buckwheat Plait: Use buckwheat flour* instead of rye flour.

To shape the plait, cut the dough in half, then cut each half into 3 equal pieces. Shape the pieces into long thin 'sausages'. Take 3 'sausages', moisten one end of each with water and press together; plait, dampening the ends to join. Repeat with the remaining 3 'sausages' to make 2 loaves. Sprinkle with 1 teaspoon whole buckwheat* instead of caraway seeds.

Leave to rise in a warm place for 30 minutes, until doubled in size. Bake in a preheated hot oven, 220°C (425°F), for 10 minutes, then lower the heat to 190°C (375°F), and bake for a further 15 to 20 minutes. Cool on a wire rack.

DRESSINGS AND SAUCES

SHOYU DRESSING

¾ cup oil
2 tablespoons shoyu*
2 tablespoons lemon juice
2 cloves garlic
pepper

Place all the ingredients in a screw-topped jar and shake well to blend.
Makes 1¼ cups

Ginger Dressing: Add a 2.5 cm (1 inch) piece finely chopped root ginger to the ingredients.

FRENCH DRESSING

¾ cup olive oil
4 tablespoons wine
* vinegar*
1 teaspoon Meaux
* mustard*
1 clove garlic, crushed
1 teaspoon clear honey
salt and pepper

Put all the ingredients in a screw-topped jar, adding salt and pepper to taste. Shake well before serving.
Makes 1 cup

Vinaigrette Dressing: Add 2 tablespoons chopped mixed herbs – such as mint, parsley, chives, chervil or thyme – to the above ingredients.

GREEN HERB DRESSING

30 g (1 oz) parsley
15 g (½ oz) mint
15 g (½ oz) chives
3 sorrel leaves, chopped
⅔ cup natural yogurt
2 tablespoons olive oil
juice of ½ lemon
1 teaspoon clear honey
½ teaspoon salt
¼ teaspoon pepper

Remove the stalks from the parsley and mint. Place the leaves in an electric blender or food processor with the remaining ingredients and blend until smooth.

Store in the refrigerator for up to one week. Shake before use.
Makes 1¼ cups

TOMATO SAUCE

2 tablespoons olive oil
1 onion, chopped
1 clove garlic, crushed
500 g (1 lb) tomatoes,
    skinned and chopped
2/3 cup vegetable stock
2 teaspoons tomato paste
1 bay leaf
salt and pepper

Heat the oil in a pan, add the onion and fry for 5 minutes, until softened. Add the remaining ingredients, with salt and pepper to taste, cover and simmer for 20 minutes, stirring occasionally.

Cool slightly and remove the bay leaf. Work in an electric blender or food processor until smooth, or rub through a sieve. Reheat gently.
Makes 1½ cups

MUSHROOM SAUCE

2 tablespoons oil
1 onion, chopped
1 clove garlic, crushed
125 g (4 oz) mushrooms,
    chopped
1 tablespoon wholemeal
    flour
1/3 cup vegetable stock
1/3 cup milk
2 teaspoons shoyu*
salt and pepper

Heat the oil in a pan, add the onion and fry until softened. Add the garlic and mushrooms and cook for about 2 minutes. Stir in the flour, then remove from the heat and stir in the stock and milk. Bring to the boil, stirring, and cook for 3 minutes. Stir in the shoyu, and seasoning to taste.

Cool slightly, then work in an electric blender or food processor until smooth. Reheat gently.

Serve with nut roasts and rissoles.
Makes 2 cups

PIQUANT SAUCE

2/3 cup natural yogurt
1 teaspoon tomato paste
1/2 teaspoon cumin powder
1 teaspoon ground
    coriander
1 teaspoon clear honey

Place all the ingredients in a small bowl and mix together thoroughly.
Makes 2/3 cup

INDEX

ACKNOWLEDGMENTS

Recipes devised and food prepared by Carole Handslip
Photography by Roger Phillips
Photographic Stylist: Gina Carminati